A Cure for a Scold

by James Worsdale

1735

A FACSIMILE PUBLISHED BY CORNMARKET PRESS
FROM THE COPY IN THE BIRMINGHAM SHAKESPEARE LIBRARY
LONDON
1969

PUBLISHED BY CORNMARKET PRESS LIMITED
42/43 CONDUIT STREET LONDON W1R ONL
PRINTED IN ENGLAND BY FLETCHER AND SON LIMITED NORWICH

SBN 7191 0179 4

A

CURE

FOR A

SCOLD.

A

Ballad FARCE

OF

Two ACTS.

(Founded upon SHAKESPEAR's *taming of a Shrew)*

As it is Acted by his Majesty's Company of Comedians at the Theatre Royal in *Drury-Lane.*

By *J. WORSDALE*, Portrait-Painter.

L O N D O N:
Printed for L. GILLIVER, at *Homer's* Head, *Fleetstreet.*
(Price One Shilling.)

To the Honourable

Edward Walpole, Efq;

S I R,

I F I have any Pleafure in publifhing the following fhort Performance, it arifes from thinking that it gives me an Opportunity of expreffing my Gratitude to you, for Favours of which my prefent happy Condition is the beft Proof.

I know, to generous Minds, like yours, even the Acknowledgment of Benefactions is unacceptable; yet I fhou'd think it hard, to be depriv'd of the Honour of declaring thofe Obligations, which would be Ingra-

titude

titude to conceal; and which I can never have any Prospect or Possibility to return.

I shall think it a peculiar Felicity, if this Attempt escapes with your Approbation, who are as excellent a Judge of Books, as of Men; and I must depend upon that same Good-nature, which hitherto has been so often employ'd in my Interest, to over-look the Imperfections both of the Author and his Productions, and to accept of this as an Instance of that Duty and Respect which you have a Right to demand from,

S I R,

Your most oblig'd,

and most devoted,

humble Servant,

James Worsdale.

THE

PREFACE.

A Young Author who ventures into the World, especially on the Stage, may very reasonably expect Ill-nature, Censure and Envy to rise up against, and make him repent of his Undertaking; but as I have prepar'd my self to expect this Treatment, I shall feel the less Uneasiness from its Attacks. It is the Fate even of the best Writers to be persecuted with Satire and Malice, and if I find the ill-natur'd Part of the World over liberal of their Aspersions, it will make me imagine, the following Performance

to

The PREFACE.

to be of more Consequence than as yet I am by any Means inclin'd to believe.

There is one great Objection, I own, against me, which is, that being by Profession a Painter, I should attempt any thing alluding to Wit or Humour; I cannot indeed justify my Conduct in this Particular by the present Practice of most of my Brethren of the Pencil, altho' Wit, Humour and Learning were not so uncommon among the Artists of Antiquity. The drawing of Characters in human Life is very near of Kin to that of painting Resemblances ; the first is a Picture of the Soul, the latter (shou'd be) of the Body and Mind together ; so that I cannot be said in the least to wander from my Profession.

If the Publick are so kind to believe that the Great Author, whose Work I have attempted to abbreviate, is not

ex-

The PREFACE.

extreamly injur'd by this Undertaking, my greatest Fear is over. I flatter myself the good-natur'd Part of Mankind will make some favourable Allowances for this first Attempt, by which generous Treatment I may perhaps be encourag'd to offer something entirely new and original.

P R O-

PROLOGUE.

L O N G has our Stage with Foreign Wit
   been cloy'd,
  And British *Authors annually employ'd,*
To alter, mend, tranfpose, tranflate and fit
Moliere'*s gay Scenes to pleafe an* English *Pit,*
Like Botching Taylors, whofe whole Merit lies
In changing Suits to different Shapes and Size.

 Our Fops and Stages fhine, to our Difgrace,
Gay with French *Wit, and gaudy with* French *Lace;*
Britain *in both an Excellence hath fhown,*
And boafts more rich Materials of her own.

 To prove this true, fee Shakefpear'*s Shrew revive,*
A Leffon, to inftruct us how to wive:
If fimple, from her Faults how beft to fhame her,
Or, if we catch a Fury, how to tame her.
'*Tis* Shakefpear *fpeaks, let ev'ry Ear attend,*
The Good we're fure to pleafe----the Bad may mend.

*Dramatis Personæ.

M E N.

Sir William Worthy ⎤   ⎡ Mr. *Shepard.*
Mr. Manly | | Mr. *Mecklin.*
Heartwell | | Mr. *Efte.*
Gainlove   ⎬ by ⎨ Mr. *Crofs.*
Archer | | Mr. *Salway.*
Phyfician | | Mr. *Harper.*
Barber   ⎦   ⎣ Mr. *Hallam.*

W O M E N.

Peg   ⎱   ⎰ Mrs. *Clive.*
Flora   ⎬ by ⎨ Mrs. *Pritchard.*
Lucy   ⎰   ⎱ Mrs. *Crofs.*

The Reader is defired to take Notice,

That A I R V. *Altho' I am a Country Lafs,* in Page 14. is to be left out ; it being plac'd there by Miftake.

A

CURE for a SCOLD.

SCENE I.

Sir *William Worthy*, *Heartwell*.

Sir *W*. RESS me no more, Mr. *Heartwell*, with your Importunity, I am finally determin'd, not to permit any Addreſses to my youngeſt Daughter, before I have provided a Husband for my Eldeſt : If thou canſt have any ſerious Thoughts about her, court her, thou ſhalt have her, and a Portion ſufficient to gild all her Imperfections.

Heart. Why, Sir *William*, I had as good be wedded to a continual Tempeſt, the Sea in all its Fury, is leſs turbulent and reſtleſs than her Spirit.

B

Sir

Sir W. And therefore, I wou'd be at an extraordinary Expence to get her off my hands.

Heart. Expence ! why, what Bribe will be fufficient to tempt a Purchafer ? I would as foon take her Dowry, to be lafh'd by the Hangman publickly once a Week.

A I R I.   Lillybullero.

The fharpeft of Plagues that Satan cou'd find,
To torture, perplex and embitter our Life ;
Is certainly this to be link'd and confin'd,
'Till Death—to a termagant Jade of a Wife.
   If Wealth fhe brings,
   She flaunts and flings,
Difpleafing and teizing, ill-natur'd and
   Her felf only prizing, (*proud ;*
   Her Husband defpifing,
As Silver in Bells makes 'em doubly as loud.

Sir W. Nay ! you know my determin'd Refolution, and if ever thou feeft my Daughter *Margaret* married, thou fhalt have the moft favourable Admiffion to her Sifter ; 'till then I defire you may defift.   [*Exit.*

Heart. Was ever Mortal in fuch diftrefsful Circumftances as I am ? prohibited all approach to the Objeﬄ of my Wifhes—— unlefs fome defperate Man can be found, to hazard a Match with a female Monfter. What, tho' her Father be rich, will any Man knowingly fwallow Poifon, becaufe the
Pill

Pill is gilded ? I doubt it——and yet upon
Recollection, there may be good Fellows in
the World, if a Man knew where to light
on 'em, who wou'd take her with all her
Faults and——Money enough.

AIR II. *White Joke.*

A Woman, tho' never so ugly and old,
So crooked, so curst, and so crabbed a Scold,
Finds plenty of Lovers, for plenty of Gold:
For Marriages now are no more than a Trade,
And Mortals will drudge to be handsomely
On Sea, or Shore,   (paid.
To swell their Store,
Men dig in a Mine, or tug at an Oar,
Or wed, which is worse—O! what Asses
(we're made?

Enter Manley, Archer.

But if I mistake not, my Friend *Manley*
comes this way : What happy Gale blows
you to *London* ? why in this Habit, why in
Mourning ?

Man. A common Calamity to us young
Men, my Father has been dead these four
Months.

Heart. Poor old Gentleman ! I'm griev'd
for him.

Arch. If the Grief of the Living cou'd
really recall the Dead, I believe few Heirs
wou'd thank their Friends for unreasonable
Lamentation.

Man.

Man. Hither, *Heartwell*, I come, to try my Fortune, to fee if good Luck and my Friends will help me to a Wife——Will you aſſiſt me in this Affair?

Heart. What Qualifications will you expect?

Man. Why Money, a good Portion.

Heart. Is that all?

Man. That all! Why a good Fortune has every kind of Good contain'd in it.

Heart. If thoſe be your Sentiments, your Deſires may ſpeedily be ſatisfy'd; to deal truly, I cou'd point you out a Wife, and a rich one too; but thou'rt too much my Friend, I will not wiſh thee ſuch a one—— her Face.

Man. Oh, that ſhall break no Squares, ſo ſhe be but rich.

Heart. She's rich, young, and beautiful; but ſhe has a Temper ſhrewd and froward, and a Tongue more turbulent and noiſy than an Iron Mill.

Man. Piſh, a Trifle, a very Trifle. Prithee who is it?

Heart. Since thou art ſo deſperate, I'll tell thee; her Father is Sir *William Worthy*, her Name is *Margaret*, and the whole Town is acquainted with the Merit of her Tongue.

Man. The Town's an Aſs; come, ſhew me the Houſe, I will not ſleep, 'till I woo her and win her; her Father knows me well, and I believe has ſome Knowledge
of

of my Fortune ; nay, I'm refolv'd, Man, come, nay, prithee come.   [*Exeunt.*

Enter Margaret, Flora.

Marg. Marry come up, you proud Slut, muft you be making your felf fine before your eldeft Sifter, you're the Favourite, are you ? but I fhall make you know your Diftance, I'll teach you your Duty to your Elders, Huffy, I will——give me that Fan, and that Handkerchief ; there, take that——'tis good enough for you.

Flo. Here, take 'em, Sifter—I refign 'em freely ; I wou'd gladly give you all I have, to purchafe your Kindnefs.

Marg. Ah, you flattering Gipfey, I cou'd find in my Heart to flit your diffembling Tongue.

Flo. You wrong me, Sifter—my Tongue has been always my Heart's Interpreter.

AIR III. *Did not you hear of a Jovial Sailor.*

'Tis Man alone fo fubtle wife is,
   To act a falfe diffembling Part ;
The Virgin's Thought without Difguife is,
   Her very Eyes unveil her Heart.
Then think, O! think, what killing Anguifh,
   The faithful Heart when doubted knows ;
Unkind Sufpicions make it languifh,
   As Heats unkind deftroy the Rofe.

Marg.

Marg. No more fquawling, Miftrefs, I fee you are over-run with Impertinence, becaufe you have a Lover or two: I fuppofe you are dying for *Heartwell*; tell me, or I will pinch thee like a Fairy. ''

Flo. If you efteem him, Sifter, I vow to plead for you myfelf, but you fhall have him.

Marg. What, Huffey, fhall I have your Leavings?   [*Curt'fies.*

Enter Worthy.

Sir *W.* Why how now? whence grows this Infolence? *Flora*, get thee in poor Girl——fhe weeps, fye *Peg*, put off this devilifh Humour, I'm fure fhe never crofs'd thee.

Marg. Her Silence flouts me, and I'll be reveng'd.   [*flies at her.*

Sir. *W.* What, in my fight too, you ill-natur'd thing; go *Flora*, get thee out of her way.   [*Exit* Flora.

Marg. Muft I be hinder'd! nay, now I fee fhe's the Favourite, fhe muft have a Hufband —— I fee your Care of me, but I'll find a way to be reveng'd.   [*Exit.*

Sir *W.* Was ever poor Man thus plagu'd?

Enter

Enter Manley, Heartwell, Archer.

But who's here? my Friend *Heartwell!*

Heart. Ay, Sir, ſoon return'd, you ſee, I have brought my Friend *Manley* to ſee you.

Man. Your moſt humble Servant, Sir.

Sir *W. Manley,* you are welcome, I hear you have loſt your Father lately.

Man. 'Tis true, Sir, but I hope to find another in you; I hear you have a fair Daughter, call'd *Margaret,* you know my Fortune, and if you like my Perſon, with your Conſent, I'll be your Son-in-law.

Sir *W.* I have indeed ſuch a Daughter, but I have ſo great a Regard for you, that I wou'd not put her into your Hands——ſhe'll make you mad.

Arch. As for that matter, he's mad e-nough already; Sir, he wants no new Me-dicine to make him more ſo.

Man. Sirrah, you long to have your Bones broke——I'll venture it, Father——for ſo I'll preſume to call you; I am as peremp-tory as ſhe's wilful, and where two raging Fires meet, they muſt conſume whatever feeds their Fury; then tell me, if I get your Daughter's Conſent, what Portion will you give?

Sir *W.* After my Death, one half of my Eſtate, and on the Wedding-Day ten thou-ſand Pounds.

Man.

Man. And I'll affure her, an equal Jointure ; get but the Writings drawn, I'll engage to win her Confent.

Sir *W.* I wifh thee Succefs, with all my heart ; will you go with us, or fhall I fend my Daughter to you ?

Man. Oh! fend her by all means. [*Ex.*

Heart. Why, *Manley*, this is a moft defperate Venture.

Man. Not in the leaft —— not in the leaft —— why, fay fhe rail, I'll fwear fhe fings, as fweet as a Nightingale ; or fhou'd fhe frown, I'll fay, fhe's as mild as a Summer's Sky——if filent, I'll commend her Volubility ; and, if fhe fcorns to wed me, I'll ask what Hour fhe'll fix to join our Hands——But, here fhe comes, leave me *Heartwell.*

Enter Margaret.

Sweet *Peg*, my pretty, pretty *Peg*, how doft thou do ?

Mar. Marry come up, Sauce-Box—— plain *Peg*, where have you left your Breeding ? if ever you had any : I am called Madam.

Man. No, no, *Peg*, thou ly'ft, thou'rt call'd plain *Peg*, and bonny *Peg*, and fometimes *Peg* the curft, take this from me ; hearing thy Mildnefs mentioned every where, thy Virtues fpoke of, and thy

Beautys

Beautys praifed ; I come to woo thee
Peg, to be my Wife.

Marg. So fhou'd I be fure to have a fcur-
vy Bargain.

Man. Why, now I fee the World has
much abus'd thee ; 'twas told me, thou
wert rough, and wild, and fullen, but I
find nothing in thee, but Mildnefs and Good-
Nature ; I fee thou canft not frown, nor
pout, nor bite the Lip, like other angry
Wenches, thou'rt all Sweetnefs, *Peg*.

Marg. Don't provoke me, Sir, I won't
ftand quiet to hear my felf abus'd.

Man. What Rogue was he, that told me
thou wert lame ; thou art as ftrait, *Peg*, as
an Ofier, and as pliable ; that Air, that
Walk, becomes thee to a Miracle.

Marg. Does it fo, Jackanapes ? how will
a Halter become you, with a running Knot
under one Ear ?

Man. Nay, no Knot, *Peg*, but the
Knot of Matrimony, between thee and
me.

Arch. Now, let me be hai r, if I know
which Knot is worft ; yet were I to chufe,
I think the running Knot would be the
beft, becaufe one might foon be out of
one's Pain in fuch a Cafe : I like not your
Knots, that a Man is all his Life-time wifh-
ing to untie, and to no purpofe.

C   *Marg.*

Marg. I will not ſtay to be mock'd, by ſuch crack-brain'd Fellows.

Man. Nay, ſtay *Peg*, prithee ſtay ——— in faith, you ſtir not yet ; I tell thee, in plain Terms, that I have thy Father's Conſent ; your Portion's agreed upon, your Jointure ſettled, the Writings are drawn, and for your own part, be willing or unwilling, all's one, you and I will marry, I'm reſolv'd on't.

Marg. What, without my Leave, Impudence ?

Man. A Fig for your Leave,——here's a Clatter with a noiſy Woman——be contented, for I'll have it ſo.

Marg. You ſhall be hang'd firſt——you ſhall——within there.

Man. No Noiſe, *Peg* ; get me a Stick, *Archer* ; by this Hand, deny to promiſe me before your Father, and I'll not leave you a whole Rib ; I'll make you do it, and be glad on't.

Marg. Why, you will not murder me, I hope ? you are a Couple of Raſcals, I don't doubt, but you wou'd pick my Pocket.

Arch. I have a ſtronger Temptation, to pick your Tongue out of your Head, an it were but as eaſily done.

Marg. Take that, Puppy, and ſpeak next when it comes to your turn.

Man.

Man. Come, come, leave thefe Frolicks; have you, I will, or no Man ever fhall——whoe'er attempts it, I'll be the Death of him, before he lies one Night with thee ; perhaps, of thee too, to bear him Company ; 'tis I am come to tame thee.

Enter Worthy, Heartwell.

Here comes your Father——never deny me, for if you do, you know what follows.

Marg. The Devil's in this Fellow, he has beat me, at my own Weapons ; now, have I a mind to marry him, to try if I can't tame him.

Sir *W.* Well, *Manley*——what Succefs with my Daughter ?

Man. It is impoffible I fhou'd fpeed a-mifs ; fhe's the beft-natur'd Lady.

Sir *W.* Why, how now, Daughter, in the Dumps ?

Marg. You fhew a Father's Care, indeed, to match me to fuch a mad hectoring Fellow.

Man. She has been flander'd grievoufly, fhe is not curft, unlefs for Policy ; and for Patience, fhe's a fecond *Grizel* ; between us, we have agreed to have the Wedding in an Hour's time.

Marg. I'll fee you hang'd firft.   [*Afide.*

Heart. Hark ye —— *Manley* —— fhe fwears, fhe'll fee you hang'd firft.

Man. Pifh, that's but her way of talking, we have made a Bargain, that before Company, fhe fhall maintain, fome of her extravagant Humours; for fhe muft not feem to fall off from it too foon; when we are alone, we are as fond as two Turtles. Well, Father, provide the Feaft, invite your Guefts, and I will juft ftep to my Lodging to fettle fome Affairs, and return immediately. Give me thy Hand, *Peg.*

Marg. Why, Sir, Sir, do you mean to marry me in fpite of my teeth?

Man. No Words, *Peg,* no Words—— thou need'ft not be peevifh before Friends—— 'tis only before Strangers, according to the Bargain; come, *Peg,* thou fhalt fee me to the Door.——

Marg. As I live, I will not.

Man. By this Light, but you fhall—nay, no tefty Tricks,

[*Exeunt.*

Heart. A little fhort Moment did *Man-ly* debate,

Within his great Bofom, this Crifis of Fate;

Then, like a brave *Cæfar,* he threw the bold Caft,

And ftrait over Wedlock's Life Rubicon paft.

Was ever Match clapt up fo fuddenly?

Sir *W.*

Sir *W.* Faith, never——becaufe, perhaps fuch a Couple never met : I have ventur'd madly, but he's a Gentleman of an extraordinary Character.

Heart. I don't doubt, but you'll think your felf happy in him ; efpecially, if he mends her Temper : but a Woman's Temper is like Wine, there are many ways to make it fharp, but not one to make it palatable——if it be naturally four.

Sir *W.* That's very true, Sir.

AIR IV.　*Of all the fimple Things we do.*

That Man may well defpair, who tries,
　To fup up the Sea with a Spoon;
To mend a bad Wife, is a Tryal as wife,
　And may be effetted as foon.
Three ways, a Philofopher faith,
　A Scold may be cur'd if fhe's young :
　　　To ftop her Breath,
　　　Or fret her to Death,
Or fnip off the Tip of her Tongue.

Sir. *W.* 'Tis e'en fo——but let's in, to prepare Things againft the Wedding.
　　　　　　　　　　　　　[*Exeunt.*

Entet

Enter Flora, Lucy.

Flo. So, I think, all Matters are agreed on, *Lucy.*

Lu. Yes, Madam, and as I was ſaying, you know, he is certainly twice as mad as ſhe——but, as I ſay, it will be my Lady's turn next——and, you may now e'en chuſe where you like.

Flo. I ſhall not be very ready to determine, *Lucy :* It is a Matter that requires a great deal of Caution.

A I R V.　*Altho' I am a Country Laſs.*

Altho' ſo fondly Men profeſs,
*　　To love us without ranging ;*
Their Paſſions vary, like their Dreſs,
*　　Decaying, ever changing.*

No Face ſo fair, no Eye ſo bright,
*　　From roving to reſtrain them ;*
As Boys whom gilded Toys delight,
*　　Poſſeſs, and then diſdain them.*

Lu. That's what I ſay, Madam——and, I ſaid it to his Face, Madam ——juſt now ;
when

when he was plaguing me, to let him fee
you, for faid I, my Lady defpifes you
all———and, as I fay, all you Lovers may
e'en go hang your felves for her————
and————

Flo. But hold, *Lucy* ; you fpoke all
this without my Direction.

Lu. Why, ay, Madam, that's true————
but, you know, as I fay, where one loves,
one's apt to fpeak heartily.

Flo. And, pray who was this Perfon
that was plaguing you fo ?

Lu. Only Mr. *Gainlove*————he faid,
he was fure you wou'd not be difpleas'd
at his Admittance ; but I knew to the
contrary, and fo I told him roundly ————
indeed, it pity'd the Heart of me, to fee
the poor Gentleman figh, and wrap his
Hands a-crofs his Breaft, and lift up his
Eyes, and hang down his Head,————
and, as I was faying, it griev'd the Heart
of me, to let him go————but, to pleafe
you, Madam————

Flo. Perhaps, 'twou'd have pleas'd me
more to have admitted him.

Lu. O Lord, Madam ! there's no harm
done, I'll warrant, he's within call————
ay, ay, when a body knows your Mind, as
I fay, then one knows what to do ; ay, ay,
I'll fetch him.

Flo.

Flo. Stay, *Lucy*, now thou'rt as much too officious.

Lu. Nay, in good faith, will I not——
I am refolv'd to pleafe your Ladyfhip.
[*Exit.*

Flo. I fee, it's impoffible to conceal an Affection, when once it has taken poffeffion of us.

A I R VI.   *Down in the North Country.*

How vain's our Scorn, and Woman's Pride,
   Our Paffion to conceal ;
When what we ftudy moft to hide,
   Our Actions moft reveal.

The Bird whofe trembling Breaft,
   Pants for its Young, afraid ;
By fearing to difclofe her Neft,
   Is by thofe Fears betray'd.

Enter

Enter Lucy, Gainlove.

Lu. Nay, Madam, 'tis too late as I fay, to counterfeit, I have e'en told him all, and fhall leave it to yourfelves to agree. [*Exit.*

Gain. Forgive me, *Flora*, for this Intrufion, let me not defpair, fince the Sincerity and Ardour of my Affections demand fome Return.

Flo. You know how abfolute my Father's Commands are not to receive any Addreffes till my elder Sifter is marry'd.

Gain. Then, my fair One, you'll be foon at Liberty, for every Thing I hear is ready, and they are only waiting for the Bridegroom.

Flo. It is neceffary then for me to retire for fear of my Father's difcovering us.

Gain. Only give me Leave to tell you, that your Father defigns to marry you to *Heartwell* To-morrow, and therefore you muft be fpeedy in your Determination ; I flatter myfelf that I am not wholly indifferent to you, and if I am really fo happy, let us not both be facrific'd.

Flo. I dare not ftay to anfwer you now, you fhall know my Refolution To-night. *Lucy* will conduct you to me, and we may have a better Opportunity of fettling Affairs, while the Family are employ'd about my Sifter.

D

Gain.

Gain. Till then I shall be miserable.
[*Manet* Flora.

A I R VII. *Wally,* &c.

Flora.   *Altho' so fondly Men profess*
to love us, without ranging,
Their Passions vary like their Dress,
decaying, ever changing.

No Face so fair, no Eye so bright,
From roving to restrain them ;
As Boys, whom gilded Toys delight,
possess, and then disdain them.

Enter Worthy, Heartwell, Margaret, Manley, Archer.

Man. I thank your Friends for your Attendance, I know you think to sup with me To-night, but Business of the utmost Consequence obliges me to take my Leave.

Sir *Wm.* Is't possible you will away To-night ?

Man. I must immediately, if you knew my Business you wou'd not wonder at my abrupt Departure. Again, I thank you all who have beheld me give away myself to this most patient, mild and gentle Wife, sup with my Father, here, and drink my Health, for I must hence. So farewell to you all.

Heart.

Heart. Let me intreat you to ſtay till after Supper.

Man. It muſt not be.

Heart. Let me prevail with you.

Man. 'Tis impoſſible.

Mar. Let me intreat you.

Man. I'm content.

Mar. Are you content to ſtay?

Man. I am content you ſhou'd intreat me, but ſtay I will not, intreat me how you can.

Mar. Now if you love me.

Man. I cannot; *Archer,* the Horſes.

Arch. They have not eat their Wedding Supper, Sir.

Man. Sirrah, get the Horſes.

Mar. Nay then do what thou can'ſt, I will not go neither To-night, nor To-morrow, nor till I pleaſe myſelf: The Door is open, Sir; there lies your Way.

AIR VIII. *Red Houſe.*

Wives will be inſulted,
 if ſo tame to bear it;
Husbands will be Tyrants,
 proudly they declare it;
Women ſhou'd remind 'em
 of their humble Duty,
Nature has deſign'd 'em
 Slaves to Love and Beauty.

I will affert my Sex's Right,
  his Noife and Frowns alike defpife,
Since angry Wives like Vipers bite,
  let none provoke them if they're wife.

Man. Peg, be content,—— I pr'ythee be not angry.

Mar. I will be angry if I pleafe. Father, be quiet, he fhall ftay my Leifure.

Heart. Ay, now fhe begins to fhow her-felf.

Mar. Gentlemen, forward to the Bridal Supper; I fee a Woman may be made a Fool of, if fhe wants a little Spirit.

Man. They fhall go forward, *Peg,* at thy Command; obey the Bride, you that attend on her; go to the Feaft, carouze, be mad or merry; but for my bonny *Peg,* fhe muft with me; nay, look not big upon't, nor ftamp, nor ftare, nor fret; fhe is my Property, my Goods, my Chattels, and I will be the Mafter of my own. Look, here fhe ftands, touch her who dare; I'll make him fmoke that ftops me. Fear not, *Peg,* I'll guard thee againft a Million. ——Nay, come.

Mar. Will none of you help me. [*Exit.*

Sir *Wm.* Nay, let 'em go;——they are a Couple of quiet ones however; let's fpend the Evening chearfully, and to make it look fomewhat like a Wedding, we will have
the

the Dance that was intended. Within there, let the Dancers come in.

A DANCE.

By this Time I believe we are expected to Supper. I'll shew you the Way.   [*Exit.*

End of the First Act.

ACT II. SCENE I.

Enter Peter, Archer.

Pet. HONEST *Archer*, welcome.

Arch. Are all Things ready according to your Orders?

Pet. They are. Are my Master and his Wife near?

Arch. Just by,——have you a large Fire, for it is bitter cold.

Pet. Ev'ry Thing's in Order; but is she as peevish a Scold as she is reported.

Arch. She was before the Frost,——but thou knowest such Weather as this tames Man and Beast.

Pet. Why ay that's true, —— then is a Scold worse than a Beast, —— for I ne'er heard that the coldest Weather cou'd tame such sort of Cattle; many a Night has my Wife been out in Frost and Snow, yet I ne'er found her a whit the better for it. But tell me some News of our new Mistress.

Arch.

Arch. I fancy ſhe had her Education at *Billingſgate,* and my poor Maſter I fear will lead a Dog's Life with her; for ſhe ſeems to me to have Mercury at her Fingers End.

A I R I. *The Twitcher.*

I.

Whoe'er, to a Wife
Is link'd, for his Life,
Is plac'd in moſt wretched Condition:
   Tho' plagu'd with her Tricks,
   Like a Bliſter ſhe ſticks,
And Death is his only Phyſician,
And Death is his only Phyſician,
           Poor Man!

II.

To trifle and toy,
May give a Man Joy,
When ſummon'd by Love, or by Beauty;
   But, where is the Bliſs in
   Our Conjugal Kiſſing,
When Paſſion is prompted by Duty.
When Paſſion is prompted by Duty.
           Poor Man!

III.

The Cur who poſſeſs'd
Of Mutton the beſt,
A Bone he cou'd leave at his Pleaſure:
               But,

But, if to his Tail
'Tis ty'd, without Fail
He's harraſs'd and plagu'd beyond Meaſure.
He's harraſs'd and plagu'd beyond Meaſure.

          Poor Cur!
        [*Exit* Archer.

Enter Manley, Margaret.

Man. Where are theſe Knaves? what no more Slaves to hold my Stirrups, nor to take my Horſe. *Peter, James, Ralph, Gregory.*

      Enter Servants.

All. Here, here, Sir.
Man. Here, Sir, here, Sir,——ye Loggerheads, Puppies, what no Attendance, no Regard, no Duty, ye ſlothful Knaves, be gone and fetch my Supper in; Rogues, do I ſpeak, and don't ye flye; ſit down *Peg,* and welcome,—— nay, good ſweet *Peg,* be merry when I bid thee,——theſe are Country Clowniſh Fellows. Pr'ythee be merry. —off with my Boots, Sirrah. Ye Rogues, ye Villains.

Mar. Sure he will run himſelf out of Breath, and then it will be my Turn to ſpeak.

Man. Out, ye Rogue, you pluck my Boot awry; take that, and mind the pulling off the other. Be merry, *Peg.* Some
                       Water

Water here, ho——Where are my Slippers?
Shall I have some Water?——Stay, Rogues,
Draw on my Boots again. —— Come, *Peg*,
wash and welcome. You Whoreson Villain,
will you let it fall?

Mar. 'Twas an unwilling Fault.

A I R II. *Joan be not so coy.*

Man. *Peg, be not so shy.*
  Tol, lol, lol, derol.
  None loves you better than I.
  Tol, lol, lol.

Mar. *Fool, be not so vain.*
  Tol, lol, derol.
  I'll have my Turn to reign.
  Tweedledum, Tweedledum.

Man. *Peg, I'll use thee well.*
  Tol, lol, lol, derol.
  But hope not to bear the Bell.
  Tol, lol, lol, derol.

Mar. *I'll be snubb'd by none,*
  Tol, lol, lol, derol.
  I'll break your Heart or my own.
  Tweedledum, Tweedledum.

Man. Come, *Peg*, sit down,—— I know
you have a Stomach; come, fall too and
welcome——sweet *Peg*——What's this, Mutton?

Serv. Yes, Sir.
Man. Who bought it?
Serv. I, Sir.

    E   *Man.*

Man. You, Sir.——Why, Rafcal, 'tis a Piece of a Dog ; it has not the leaft Look of Mutton ; 'tis fhrivell'd and burnt to a Cinder.——Where is the Cook ? How dare you bring fuch rotten Meat to my Table, d'ye mean to poifon me, ye Joltheads ?

Mar. Pray, Husband, be content, the Meat's good Meat, and I'm hungry ; I muft and will eat fome of it.

Man. Not for the World, *Peg,*——I love thee better than fo, 'tis burnt, and will breed Choler, and we are both too full of Choler already---I love thee too well to give thee any thing to hurt thee,—we'll faft To-night,To-morrow we fhall be better furnifh'd.

Mar. Say what you will, Sir, I'll eat fome of it ; was I brought hither to be ftarv'd ?

Man. Why, you ill-natur'd Rafcals, will you ftand ftill, and fee your Miftrefs poifon herfelf; take it out of her Sight. [*Sends the Meat away.*] Well, *Peg,* this Night we'll faft for Company. Come, I'll fhew, thee to thy Bed-chamber.

Mar. I muft eat fomething, or elfe I fhall be fick ; thefe two Days have I fafted at Home out of Peevifhnefs, and now I muft ftarve out of Neceffity,——but an Egg.

Man. No, no, pr'ythee don't talk on't ; to Bed upon a full Stomach——Come, *Peg.*
[*Exit.*

Arch. Did'ft ever fee the like, *Peter ?*
Pet.

Pet. Never —— he kills her in her own Humour.

Arch. He fets out well, I wifh he may hold it ; Wives and ftumbling Horfes are beft manag'd by keeping always a tight Rein ; let 'em but go their own Gate, and they'll break your Neck.

Pet. Come, *Archer*, let's drink Succefs to him for the Honour of *Englifh* Husbands, and give us a Song.

Arch. Such as I can I will, —— with all my Heart.

AIR III. *Beffy Bell.*

How fweetly glide the Hours away,
  While chearfully we're drinking ;
By Wine the Soul's made brifk and gay,
  And Courage is kept from finking.

Since Life's fo fhort, let's take our Swing,
  Let Bacchus *reign ador'd, Sir,*
Who makes the Slave as bleft as a King,
  And the Beggar as great as a Lord, Sir.

Who makes, &c.
  And the Beggar, &c.

Where are you, Rogues ? *Peter, Ralph, Archer.*   [*Within.*

Arch. Let's away, or we fhall be all ruin'd.   [*Exit.*

S C E N E *draws, and difcovers a Bed.*

Enter Manley, Margaret.

Man. Where are thefe idle Knaves?
Some Lights there. —— Come, *Peg*, un-
drefs to Bed.

Enter Servants.

Mar. Pray fend your Men away, and
fend for fome of your Maids.

Man. Maids! hang Maids, I've no fuch
Vermin about my Houfe,——any of thefe
will do as well.

Mar. Why do mean to treat me like a
Slave?

Man. Be content; fweet *Peg*, be content. Who made this Bed? What Rafcals
are thefe? Foh! Thefe Sheets are mufty as
the Devil, and what Rags are here? Is this
a Counterpane? 'Tis a Difh-clout.

Mar. Why, the Counterpane is well
enough, and rich enough, and the Linnen
fweet as one cou'd wifh.

Man. Fye, fye, *Peg*, thou haft got a
Cold, and haft loft thy Smelling; I tell thee
they are mufty and damp; I wou'd not
have thee lye in them for the World, it
wou'd be thy Death; we muft e'en fit up
To-night, there's no Remedy.

Mar.

Mar. Pray, Sir, talk not of fitting up, I am fo fleepy I can fcarce hold my Eyes open, I muft to Bed.

Man. Not To-night, *Peg*, I'll contrive to keep thee waking. Some Wine, ho.

[*Enter Servants, with Wine.*

Come, *Peg*, Here's to thee with all my Heart in a Bumper,——my Father's Health, *Peg*, you muft pledge it.

Mar. I can't drink without eating, I fhou'd be fick.

Man. Pifh, that's but a Whim,——come, off with it, or thou fhalt neither eat nor drink this Month.

Mar. Shall I go to Bed when I have drank it?

Man. We'll talk of that anon, *Peg*,—— fo, that's well; now to my Horfes, *Peg*; I'll be with thee inftantly.   [*Exit.*

Mar. You may ftay till your Bones ach, e'er I cry for your Company.   [*Exit.*

Re-enter Manley.

Man. Come hither, *Archer.*

Arch. Sir.

Man. Wait on your Miftrefs, fay what you will to her, and vex her, but don't touch her, and let her have no Meat I charge you.   [*Exit.*

Arch. Meat, Sir! why fhe fhan't fmell Meat.

AIR

A I R IV. *Oh ! London is a fine Town.*

Of all the Methods moſt in Vogue
  For keeping Women quiet,
'Tis beſt to let their Sleep be ſhort,
  And ſtint them in their Diet :
For Faſting keeps their Bodies fine,
  And makes their Spirits ſmall,
By Hunger Wives, like Hawks, are taught
  To know their Keeper's Call.
Oh Marriage is a ſad Scene,
  They're mad that venture in it,
Where Pleaſure ſeldom ſhews her Face,
  Repentance in a Minute.   [*Exit.*

Enter Margaret.

A I R V. *Waly, Waly.*

Alas from ev'ry Joy debarr'd,
  To what hard Fate is Woman born,
Our tender Paſſion's beſt Reward
  Is cold Contempt and killing Scorn.
For Men inconſtant as the Wind,
  Expert in falſe deluding Arts,
When moſt careſs'd, are moſt unkind,
  They only win to break our Hearts.

Mar. What, *Philip, Ralph, Richard,*
what no Body near me? *Archer,* where are
you ?

                    Enter

Enter Archer.

Arch. Here, Madam, here.

Mar. Where's your Mafter?

Arch. He's gone, Madam, juft to fee his Horfes well fed, that's all.

Mar. And in the mean time I am famifh'd. Was ever Woman us'd fo barbaroufly ? I'm kept from Meat and Sleep, and what fpites me more than all the reft, is, he pretends 'tis out of Care and Love of me ; pr'ythee, good *Archer*, can'ft thou not get me fomewhat to eat ? I care not what it is.

Arch. I were as good be hang'd ; however, 'tis a Pity a Gentlewoman fhou'd be ftarv'd in a Chriftian Country.

Mar. Here's Money for thee,—— get me but any thing, for I'm ready to faint.

Arch. What fay you to a Neat's Tongue ?

Mar. With all my Heart.

Arch. Hum. I fear it wou'd be too hard of Digeftion, and be too heavy on your Stomach fo late at Night ; what think you of fome fine fat Tripe well broil'd.

Mar. 'Tis excellent good, *Archer*, fetch it me.

Arch. I'm afraid it wou'd be too cholerick a Diet. But fuppofe you had a piece of Beef and Muftard.

Mar. I love it.

Arch.

Arch. Ay, but the Muſtard's too hot, 'tis bad for the Tongue.

Mar. Why then the Beef without it.

Arch. Nay, Beef's not good without Muſtard.

Mar. Then both, or one, or any thing thou wilt.

Arch. Why then, the Muſtard without the Beef.

Mar. Impudent inſulting Slave! Muſt I be brav'd thus by my own Servants?

A I R VI. *Happy Clown.*

Were Women wiſe, they wou'd not wed,
 Nor truſt to falſe imperious Men,
Our Joys we leave in the Marriage-Bed,
 But never reſume 'em again.
The Maiden who ventures a Husband to take,
More ſafely and wiſely might ſport with a Snake,
 For Fortune, Plague and Strife
 For ever attend a poor Wife.

Enter Manly.

Mar. Sir, pray tell me, have you a mind to make me mad? Such Uſage as this will do it effectually.   How have I injur'd you, that you behave thus inhumanely to me? Did you marry me to kill me?

Man.

Man. No, good *Peg*, no; thou know'ſt I have a great Regard for thee,——I have been juſt preparing our Horſes to go back again to *London* to your Father's.

Mar. Well, there's ſome Comfort in getting Home again, there's Meat and ſleeping Room at leaſt. Are we to ſet out now?

Man. Immediately; *Archer*, bring out the Horſes, let's ſee, 'tis now about ſix o' Clock; we ſhall be there about Suppertime.

Mar. Six o' Clock, why, 'tis Ten at leaſt.

Man. It ſhall be but ſix o' Clock before I ſet out. Why, what a Miſchief's this? Whatever I ſay or do, you are ſtill croſſing it; let the Horſes alone, *Archer*, I'll not go this three Days, nay not this Month, perhaps, and e'er I do, it ſhall be what o' Clock I pleaſe.

Mar. Nay, Sir, let not that hinder our Journey, 'tis Six, or Nine, or Twelve, or what you will; pray let's go.

Arch. Ay, ay, e'en have it what Hour you like.

Man. Very well it is ſo, get ready quickly; come, we ſhall help to mend the Mirth of the Company. Come, *Peg*.

[*Exit.*

F *Enter*

Enter Lucy, Gainlove.

Lu. Don't you plague me fo, Mr. *Gain-love*, for as I fay, Servants muft not lofe their Bread, to oblige any one ; Service is no Inheritance, as I fay, talk not to me of your Flames, and your Darts, and your Sighs, and your Flim Flams, and I don't know what myfelf. I muft not bring you together, Mr. *Gainlove*, that's poz ; and as I fay now, you know my Refolution.

[*Offers to go.*

Gain. But, *Lucy*, perhaps I may be able to give you fufficient Reafons, to eafe all your Scruples. Suppofe your Mafter fhou'd be difpleas'd, as I am fure he will not, you fhall never want as good a Provifion while I have any Fortune. Befides there are fifty other Reafons in this Purfe that will have more Weight with you.

Lu. For, as I was faying, Sir, tho' Servants ought not to lofe their Bread willing-ly, yet one ought to hazard it, as I fay, for a kind good-natur'd Gentleman as you are, when one has to do with him ; Lord, how the fweet Lady talks of you, and dreams of you, and but, as I fay, Lovers are ftrange fort of Things.

Gain. And where is this fweet Lady of yours ? I long to be admitted.

Lu.

Lu. 'Tis well you put me in mind on't, or, as I fay, I fhou'd certainly have forgot it; a bad Memory, Mr. *Gainlove*, is a very bad Thing.

Gain. A Pox of your Memory and your Impertinence. Come, *Lucy*, difpatch, you know we have no Time to lofe.

Lu. That's true; fhe'll wonder what delays you.

A I R VII. *When bright Aurelia.*

The Maiden like the Merchant fighs
    When all his Wealth's at ftake,
He views the Shore with wifhful Eyes,
And blames the Waves, the Winds and Skies,
    That anxious bid him wake.

I'll warrant me now we fhall find her in her Chamber, as melancholy, as I fay, as a Turtle Dove.

Gain. Then, dear *Lucy*, make the more Hafte.

Lu. You won't let her flip thro' your Fingers To-night, I fuppofe; but if fhe be married to fomebody elfe To-morrow, you may e'en blame yourfelves for't, as I fay, it matters not to me. —— I'll tell you, Mr. *Gainlove*, what happen'd to a young Lady and her Lover, juft in the very fame Way you are.

Gain.

Gain. No Stories now, if you love me, *Lucy.*

Lu. I always love to hearken to Reaſons, as I ſay; now can you give me any Reaſons why I ſhould make more Haſte.

Gain. Right Chamber-maid I faith, I ſee her covetous Policy. Ay, ay, as many and as good as I gave you before.

[*Gives another Purſe.*

Lu. O Lord, ay ſure, or I were ill-natur'd indeed.

A I R VIII. *Three Sheep-skins.*

Pimps, Lawyers, and Doctors, tho' Fame has re-
nown'd 'em,
And Fortune, with Wealth, and with Favour have
crown'd 'em,
  For Bribe or Fee
  As well as me,
  Will ruin all around 'em.

Come then, follow me, theſe are the Arguments none of us can reſiſt, as I ſay, come along. [*Exit.*

Enter Manley, Margaret, *and* Archer.

Mar. I'm glad we're in *London* agen, won't you go in?

Man. Firſt kiſs me, *Peg,* and I will.

      Mar.

Mar. What in the middle of the Street?

Man. Art thou afham'd of me?

Mar. Not fo, Sir, but afham'd to kifs fo openly.

Man. Why then, let's Home again; Go fetch the Horfes, evermore crofs'd and crofs'd, nothing but crofs'd.

AIR IX.   *Polwart on the Green.*

Arch. *How vain is all our Art*
      To know the tender Sex,
      Who firft enflave a faithful Heart,
      Then ftudy to perplex.
   What Rapture from their Beauty grows,
      What Anguifh from their Scorn,
    Created like the new-born Rofe
      With Sweetnefs, but a Thorn.

Mar. Nay, I will give thee a Kifs, —— nay, pray now ftay.

Man. So, this is well. Come, my fweet *Peg,* we'll in.

Enter Lucy, Flora.

Lu. Yes, Madam, he's waiting in the Garden, you've no Time to lofe; your Sifter is juft come back.

Flo. Already? Why certainly they're both mad. Ah! *Lucy,* fhou'd *Gainlove*
                    prove

prove fo furly a Husband, 'twou'd break
my Heart.

Lu. You know, Madam, well enough,
that, as I fay, when you are as peevifh as
your Sifter you may expect the fame Ufage.
But believe me, Madam, now's your Time,
while the Family are employ'd about the
Bride, do you finifh with *Gainlove* ; nay,
you muft not think now, as I fay, think
when you are together ; come, good Madam,
before any Accident hinders you.

Flo. Well, *Lucy*, I'll follow thee. [*Exit.*

Enter Margaret, Manly.

Mar. 'Tis no jefting Matter, Sir, I am
at Home now, and it fhall be my Turn to
infult ; I know how to refent ill Ufage as
well as you do to give.

Enter Heartwell.

Man. No Words, *Peg*, no Woods ; I'm
glad to fee thee old Friend *Heartwell.*

Mar. Yes, Sir, I will have Liberty to
fpeak ; you fhall have Words, and Words
enough to make your Heart ach ; you think
perhaps that you're in the Country, but
you're miftaken, Sir, the Cafe is alter'd.

Heart.

Heart. I fee but little Alteration in her for the better.

Man. Why how now, *Peg*, thou haft been drinking, fure ; I never faw thee in fo pleafant a Humour before.

Mar. I tell thee thou art a pitiful Fellow ; a Thing beneath me, which I fcorn and laugh at.——Doft thou not tremble to think how thou haft ufed me ; I muft eat nothing, forfooth, becaufe the Cook had roafted the Mutton too dry, and I muft not go to Bed becaufe the Sheets were damp.

Man. Pr'ythee, *Peg*, Peace a little, I know thou can'ft fpeak, but fpeak fparingly, or you'll have nothing to fay To-morrow.

Mar. Yes, I will talk for ever, and ftill find fomething new to plague you with ; this is Silence to what I intend ; I'll talk louder than this ev'ry Night in my Sleep.

Arch. Then the Devil fhall be your Bedfellow for me.

A I R X.   *Bobbing Joan.*

Men are all fuch lordly Fools,
They prefcribe, not act by Rules,
Like unskilful Conjurers they
Raife up Spirits, that won't obey ;

Wives

Wives fhou'd ftill
Have their Will,
Or *torment 'em Night and Day.*

I'll learn to rail at thee in all Languages.

Man. Very pretty ; pr'ythee go on ; me-thinks there's Mufick in't ; go on *Peg.*

Mar. I'll have you chain'd to a Stake at *Billingfgate,* and have you baited by the Fifh-wives.

Man. Ha, ha, ha,——witty, *Peg,* pro-ceed.

Mar. You fhall do nothing but what I bid you, you fhall know me to be your Miftrefs.

Man. Excellent, *Peg* ! on, on,——what have you no more on't.   Ha, ha, ha.

Mar. Do you laugh and be hang'd, I'll fpoil your Sport.   [*Flies at him.*

Man. Nay, *Peg,* Hands off,——I thought you wou'd not have difgrac'd your good Parts to come to Blows fo foon,——pr'ythee, chide on, thou can'ft not think what De-light I take to hear thee,——it becomes thee, *Peg* ; what tir'd already ? Talk more, and louder, and longer, and fafter, and fharper, this is nothing, *Peg.*

Mar. I'll fee you at the Devil before I'll do any thing to pleafe you, do you like it ?

Man.

Man. Extremely ; on, *Peg*, you'll cool too faſt.

Mar. Why then, mark me,---if 'twere to ſave thee from drowning or breaking thy Neck I won't ſpeak one Word more to thee theſe two Months. [*Sits ſullenly.*

Man. Nay, good *Peg*, been't ſo hard-hearted,---what, melancholy all of a ſudden, ---thou'lt break thy poor Elbow with lean-ing on that hard Table. Shall I get a Cu-ſhion for thee, *Peg ?* I fear thou art not well---Speak to her, *Heartwell.*

Heart. How are you, Madam ? What ails you ? Pray ſpeak, you've ſo vex'd her, *Manley*, ſhe'll be ſick.

Enter Archer.

Man. I know not what's the Matter with her, ſhe has the Tooth-ach,——ſee how ſhe holds her Cheek, the Wind has gotten into her Teeth, by keeping open her Mouth this cold Weather.

Heart. 'Tis not unlikely,—I have heard her complain of that Diſorder.

Man. Poor *Peg*, I pity thee, which Tooth is it ? Wilt thou have it drawn ? What ſay'ſt thou ? Thou ſhalt——run, *Archer*, and fetch the firſt Tooth-drawer thou can'ſt meet, and then immediately deſire Dr. *Spe-cifick* to come to a Lady who is taken ſud-denly ill, and in great Danger, what d'ye

G ſtand

ftand ftaring at? Run immediately, or I'll ham-ftring you. [*Exit* Archer.] The Tooth-ach, *Heartwell*, makes Fools of all the Phyficians, there's no Cure but drawing.

Heart. If this do not make her find her Tongue, fhe has certainly loft it.

Man. Alas! her Face is fo fwell'd, fhe can't fpeak.

Enter Lucy.

Lu. Well, I'm glad, Madam, as I fay, to fee your Ladyfhip return'd fo foon.

Man. But I fear fhe can't live long in the Torment fhe has at prefent—fhe's fwell'd —don't ye fee?

Lu. Swell'd, Sir? Now, as I hope to be marry'd, Sir, I can't perceive it.

Man. Not perceive it, then thou'rt blind. Pr'ythee let her alone,---you difturb her.

Enter Archer, Splinter.

Arch. The Doctor will wait on you in-ftantly, he's only prefcribing half a dozen Blifters for a fick Man, for he loves to dif-patch his Patients with all Expedition.

Man. Here, honeft Fellow, have you brought your Inftruments?

Splin. Yes, yes, Sir; a wife Man always carries his Tools about him---what muft I do?

Man.

Man. You muſt draw a Tooth for this Gentlewoman ; do it as neatly and as gently as thou can'ſt ; take care you don't break her Jaw.

Splin. I'll warrant you, Sir---I warrant you.

Arch. Hark ye, Friend, cou'd not you by Accident, or Miſtake, or ſo, whip out her Tongue inſtead of her Tooth?

Splin. Ah, Maſter, if I cou'd but do that dextrouſly, I ſhou'd not want Buſineſs in *London.*

A I R XI. *To you Fair Ladies.*

Arch. *The Tyger proves a harmleſs Brute,*
        Depriv'd of Teeth and Claws,
      But none can make a Woman mute,
        Tho' all her Teeth he draws.
    If hinder'd of the Means to bite,
    Still with her Tongue ſhe'll vent her Spight.
          With a fal, lal.

Lu. My Heart throbs like any thing now, as I ſay,---I'll e'en call my Lady's Father.
                                   [*Exit.*
Splin. Pray, Madam, open your Mouth that I may ſee which Tooth it is. [*Mar. ſtrikes him.*] What, Sir, did you ſend for me to abuſe me ?

Man. No truly, Friend; but it seems she has alter'd her Mind, she won't have it drawn now; however, here's something for your Pains. O here comes our Physician.

Enter Physician.

Splin. Brother Doctor, I am glad you are come; I wish you as good Success as I have met with all my Heart. [*Exit.*

Phy. Was that Fellow a Fool or a Madman who went out?

Arch. It may be suspected that he is either one or t'other, since he pretends to be one of the Fraternity. [*Aside.*

Man. He was only a Barber, Sir, who was call'd to draw a Tooth for this Lady--- but I find her Distemper to be of a more mortal Nature.

Phy. Why she looks ill, indeed, her whole Body and vital Faculties seem to labour under a strong Hebetation. How long has she been seiz'd thus?

Man. Within this half Hour; but she has been often possess'd with these kind of Fits before.

Phy. Poor Lady, I fear her Case is desperate. [*Physician goes to* Margaret, *and feels her Pulse.*

Man. 'Tis what we all apprehend.

AIR

AIR XII. *And a Begging we will go.*

If Lawyers and Phyſicians
  By Learning were to thrive,
They'd prove of all Conditions
  The pooreſt Rogues alive.
                And a Begging, &c.

Enter Worthy, Lucy.

Sir *Wm.* Bleſs me, my Daughter dying!
dying ſo ſuddenly. My dear, dear Daughter.

Man. Alas, alas, Sir, it it but too true---
Wou'd I cou'd have purchas'd her Life at
the Expence of my own.

Sir *Wm.* What cou'd be her Diſeaſe?

Man. I am unwilling to gueſs, but this
wiſe Gentleman will ſoon let us know what
we have to expect.

Arch. Expect! why what ſhou'd you expect when the Phyſician comes, but Death.

Phy. Dangerous Symptoms indeed, Sir,
very dangerous Symptoms.

Sir *Wm.* Will ſhe recover, Doctor?

Phy. That, Sir, is a Queſtion not to be
eaſily reſolv'd; if it be in the Power of
Medicine to raiſe her, you may depend on
my Endeavours, but

Lu. Lord ſave us, are you come to but
it already; nay, then, my poor young Lady's gone.

Phy.

Phy. Weak Spirits, Sir, weak Spirits; Nature is quite worn out in her! Where is your greateſt Pain, Madam?

Man. She is ſpeechleſs, Sir.

Sir *Wm.* My poor Daughter! I never thought to live to ſee thee ſpeechleſs.

Phy. I find we muſt proceed in the moſt violent Way ſince the animal Spirits are ſo far exhauſted; I wou'd by all Means have her Head ſhav'd immediately, and a large Bliſter apply'd, and left Delays ſhou'd be dangerous, I will have four large Bliſters on other Parts of her Body; Bliſters are excellent Evacuatives.

Sir *Wm.* Why, Doctor, ſo many Bliſters will effectually do her Buſineſs?

Phy. I intend as much; I've a Specifick which I will alſo force down her Throat, that never fails curing all Diſtempers.

Arch. I don't doubt it; for Death, who cures all Diſtempers, generally appears in the Shape of a Pill or Potion.

Phy. Sir, I have ſeen more ſurpriſing Effects from that Specifick of mine, than ever have been produced from all other Medicines;——in Gouts, Catarrhs, Rheumatick, Cephalick, Hyſterick, Paralytick, Hydropick, Phlethorick, and Epileptick Caſes it never fails; in nervous Diſorders 'tis infallible.

Man.

Man. If it cures her Diftemper, I fhall be happy ; and miferable, to be depriv'd of her.

AIR XIII. *'Twas when the Sea was roaring.*

If Death, unkind to Beauty,
  Shou'd make my Love his Prey,
'Twill be my pleafing Duty
  To languifh Life away.

Arch. My Mafter is not the only Hufband who wou'd fing to fee his Wife in a dying Condition.

Man. What not one Word yet ? By all that's good, I'll have thee blifter'd from Head to Foot, I'm determin'd, and you know I'm refolute.——Good Doctor, fince there's no Hope, but in your Specifick and Bliftering, let's lofe no Time ?

Phy. I have my Medicines here ready, you need only fend for a Surgeon to force open her Jaws with Inftruments, and, if poffible, to bleed her pretty plentifully in one of the Veins under her Tongue, and you fhall fee a furprifing Effect. Pray, Madam, let me fee your Tongue ?

[*Enter Barber with Suds, Doctor's Man with Blifter-Plaifter,* &c.

Man. As the Life of my dear Wife is at ftake, I will run for a Surgeon myfelf; I'll bring the neareft I can lay my Hands on.

Mar.

Mar. Stay, *Manly*, ſtay, —— you've conquer'd me.

All. A Miracle! a Miracle! ſhe lives.

Heart. This is a very unexpected Victory.

Man. May I believe thee, *Peg?* Art thou in earneſt?

Mar. Not Truth itſelf is truer.

Man. Then thus I make thee Maſter of myſelf, and all I have. I am infinitely oblig'd to you, Sir, for your excellent Advice, I hope you will favour me to accept.

[*Gives Money.*

Phy. O Lord, Sir! there was no need of this Kindneſs; no Need, indeed, good Sir--- however, 'tis my Rule, that from honeſt Gentlemen and Friends I never refuſe any thing; and from my Enemies, I never think I can get enough; I ſhall be always at your Command, Sir.

Man. Provided you have your Fee conſtantly.

Phy. O, Sir! that's always underſtood--- always —— Well, this is the moſt ſudden Accident I ever met with; ſuch ſudden Recoveries are of little Uſe to us; Folks ought to die, but they ought to linger. [*Aſide.*

Arch. Ah, Doctor! all this might have been prevented, if we cou'd but have prevail'd with her to take ſome of your Specifick, ſhe had never thus ſurpriz'd us by her Recovery.

Phy.

Phy. Well, next Time, Sir, then be quicker in your Application ; 'tis enough for me to direct.   [*Exit.*

Mar. You have taught me what 'tis to be a Wife, and I shall make it my Study to be obliging and obedient.

Man. My best *Peg*, we will exchange Kindness, and be each others Servants. Come, my Love, since we are thus happily reconcil'd,

Let us chearfully sport in the conjugal Noose,
And make the Tye easy we neither can loose :
For shou'd the Slip-Knot the least awkwardly wear,
As good you'd another behind the left Ear.

AIR XIV. *Excuse me.*

Man. *Raptures crown the Marriage-State,*
     When equal Affections unite 'em,
Mar. *And Women shou'd study their Joys to compleat*
     By striving how much to delight 'em,
Man.   *O how blest am I,*
Mar.   *How caress'd am I,*
     Mutually complying.
Man. *My tender Love shall never decay,*
Mar. *My Heart shall chearfully obey ;*
     All Feuds shall cease,
Man.   *Our Loves increase,*
     While Time and Life are flying.
     Oh ! how blest, &c.

Sir *Wm.* I am fo pleas'd to fee thee fen-
fible of thy Follies, that I will add another
thoufand Pound to thy Fortune,——but a-
mongft this chearful Company I wonder that
Flora does not appear.

Enter Gainlove, Flora.

Gain. I am bound now to anfwer for her
Abfence. 'Tis I have taught her to tranf-
grefs, and thus we hope Forgivenefs.

Sir *Wm.* Nay, nay, there needs noWords;
Heaven's Bleffings attend; you need not
have been fo private, Mr. *Gainlove*, your
Fortune might deferve a better in return,
than my Daughter *Flora* can bring you;
however, I am glad to fee my Daughter
guilty of no greater Imprudence. Come,
Heartwell, you muft bear this Difappoint-
ment, I'm happy to fee my Family fettled.

Heart. Sir, I lov'd *Flora*, and fhou'd
have ftudy'd to make her happy; but fince
her own Inclinations have difpofed of her
another Way, I fhall endeavour to change
the Lover to the Friend; I'm convinc'd fhe
will deferve it.

Gain.
Flor. } We fhall endeavour, Sir.

A I R.

AIR XV. *CHORUS in Porus.*

Man.   *Come, come, soft nuptial Powers,*
      Bless, bless Bridegroom and Bride,
     Let each Rapture be ours,
      Let Love always preside.
     Hence, hence Care and Distraction,
      Love's soft gentle Bands
     Creates sweet Satisfaction,
      Where he joins the Hands.
All.   *Love gives new Satisfaction*
      Where he joins the Hands.

Mar. *By* Manly *taught, let Husbands bear the Sway,*
  'Tis Man's to rule, 'tis Woman's to obey.

E P I-

EPILOGUE.

 ELL, I muſt own, it wounds me to the Heart
To act, unwomanly---ſo mean a Part.
What---to ſubmit, ſo tamely---ſo contented,
Thank Heav'n! I'm not the Thing I repreſented.
Authors ſhould ſtudy Nature, but how few
In Life reſemble theſe our Author drew:
In ev'ry Houſe ſome Obſervation ſpend,
At Weſtminſter *begin, at* Wapping *end,*
You'll find the Scene revers'd, and ev'ry Dame,
Like old Alcides,---*making Monſters tame.*

Ye Fair, who form the radiant Circle here,
Approve that Cenſure, which you cannot fear;
And left our Author ſhou'd offend the Pit,
Perhaps---he felt thoſe Plagues---of which he writ:
If ſo, no longer let his Sorrows laſt,
But with your Praiſe o'er pay his Suff'rings paſt

F I N I S.